world without end: poems

by chloe cocking

Filidh Publishing

copyright © 2023 chloe cocking
isbn 978-1-927848-96-8
first soft cover edition
filidh publishing, victoria, british columbia
filidhbooks.com

cover design by danny weeds
cover image credit: ivan ivanovič, turdus pilaris
@sivan_photography_art

do not reproduce by any means this book, or any portion thereof without written permission of the publisher.

for everyone (really)

true seeing
is an act of love
small wonder
           then
we stumble about blind

preface

i am lucky enough to have a circle of poets in my life. they are lovely humans who challenge me to grow larger, listen better, and find exactly the right word.

in march 2020, we decided that we would each write one poem a day for every day in april 2020 in honour of national poetry month.

you may recall that period was considered the height of the lockdown in many places in north america— no one out on the streets, no one travelling to work or school. i stayed inside, along with my person and my cat, in a very tiny apartment. i worked from home. i had zoom meetings. i played scrabble with my person. (cat dislikes playing scrabble, so i knew it was pointless to ask her to join in). i banged on pots and pans every night at 7 pm in support of front-line workers who were risking their lives to keep the rest of us fed and as healthy as possible.

along the way, i wrote 30 poems in 30 days. some are very obviously "covid poems". others are poems written during covid (rather than poems about covid). as i have worked on assembling this collection, i notice that all the poems have certainly impacted by the stillness, quiet, and terrifying peacefulness of those weeks. what bubbles to the surface when you coop up a poet during a pandemic? they think about things, drilling deeper ever deeper into themselves. this book contains some of the results.

table of contents

preface 3
day 38 covid pandemic 7
day 22 covid pandemic 8
day 39 covid pandemic 9
day 24 covid pandemic 10
day 26 covid pandemic 11
day 23 covid pandemic 12
milk foam 13
day 30 covid pandemic 14
day 36 covid pandemic 15
the moon, haggard 16
day 29 covid pandemic 17
day 33 covid pandemic 18
day 34 covid pandemic 19
day 41 covid pandemic 20
day 47 covid pandemic 21
day 46 covid pandemic 22
this body is not an apology 23
my body like 24
swan's market 25
tongue 26
<untitled> 27
day 48 covid pandemic 28
<untitled> 29
what it means to be a poet 30
when i encounter chaos on the blank page 31

am bit	32
why poets are excluded from parties i	33
why poets are excluded from parties ii	34
why aren't you famous she asked	35
that old intervention	37
just a game	39
today	41
unseen and	42
impermanence	43
fluid	44
where she's from	46
dead	47
50 truths i noticed after i turned 50	48
with any luck martians	58
many lives lived	59
day 49 covid pandemic	60
dropped	61
flicker	62
birbs are a lie	63
about the author	78

day 38 covid pandemic

grief can be a
small bird on a frozen rail

or
   something
             much
                    larger

until the breath is gone from your body and
                your wet eyes no longer
        see

day 22 covid pandemic

certain years
so eventful they
are regarded as pivotal in
history years when
wars and slavery ended
(did they now?)
and generational
fissures burst into
open

1918   1945   1968

2020 will join this list it will
be remembered as a
time when a million and more
people died
and we sat behind our laptops waiting
for amazon packages

day 39 covid pandemic

sun at dawn is a broken egg   easier

to view from behind a camera than with plain

eyeballs

tiny screen

3" by 5" world

day 24 covid pandemic

i will not remember

                      the rate at which people are dying

                      boredom, frustration
                      fear beating inside me like a sparrow's heart

what sticks

                      banging pans and pots @ 7
                      mailing maggie a package of yeast for her bread
                      birdsong at 6 am without any traffic

day 26 covid pandemic

my face mask says
i care enough
not to breathe on you

i want to
hold you in an agape embrace
or at least touch your arm
while you drink coffee

day 23 covid pandemic

apartment is close and stuffy
daily 7 pm cacophony
i open a window and
stand on my balcony with metal pot & wooden spoon
no one to touch
but they are out there
i hear them

milk foam

red dress purple cup sunny morning
poem in this?
yes a poem in that　　　　　beyond

moon-june-spoon

moment of almost-joy
drape of the red dress as it falls over my legs
when i sit

milk foam on my lip, on my tongue-tip when
i sip from
the purple ceramic bowl

whatever the day brings

there is still the matter of my red dress
the purple cup
sunlight across green leaves

day 30 covid pandemic

when people stayed inside like indoor cats
looking out the window at the birds

it only took a couple of days before

big horn sheep paraded through the village
families of foxes toured both sides of the boulevard
bears swam in tiny chlorinated ponds
eagles kept a watchful eye on the river

crows
those small magic kings of tree-tops and air
hectored the squirrels scurrying by

day 36 covid pandemic

note that halfway thru the challenge i
wonder when i will feel
like a real poet
as if my self-doubt
disincorporates   me

                    i am vanishing as i
write?

the moon, haggard

an unwashed slattern
slices the cold sky
like a stinging blade

a poet who has murdered
sleep

*dangerous
in other words*

is writing an invocation
full of spelling and grammar
under the sharp chill moon

can you call your poems back
when they fly like hunting bats?

day 29 covid pandemic

know this:

a hug is a kind of containment

day 33 covid pandemic

hands deep in dough
sugar soaking through my
skin as i knead then i
chop walnuts and stir

day 34 covid pandemic

twenty-seven email
one dozen banana walnut muffins
two trips to the compost
another fourteen email
wipe the counters, twice
set one pan of will-be focaccia to proof for two hours
feed the cat (just the one, the other's gone).
another nine email

day 41 covid pandemic

does anybody hot-knife hash anymore?

where are all the heat-stained blades

scraping cold margarine across crumbling toast?

day 47 covid pandemic

poem's
  like a painting

      layers of meaning
          you are tempted to fuss over it

          until you fuck it up
              and end up with dirty hands

day 46 covid pandemic

memory slips from one fiction to another, like she always does, recalling moments changed not just by time or virus in the moment they happened, wtf of whatever-it-was lost in the impulse to tell a complete story, beginning, middle and end::

this body is not an apology

call off ur dogs
find love for this shivering naked self
you and me united by vulnerabilities

the parts that don't work
the parts that don't fit
the parts infused with shame

squirming un-comfort-able
do not give it a name
this body like unbaked bread

my body like

a tertiary road map of
rural saskatchewan
 shiny scars like zippers in
too many places

all the places i've been stitched up tight
        small of my back
        all around my breasts
        across my belly from hip to hip

grafted skin patch like melted candlewax
stretch marks- from growth, from birth- in every soft place
pleated into looser flesh
shiny & tight when rounded with fat

the scar my brother made on my right wrist
the scar my lover made on my left arm
the scars i made, forehead and backofskull,
twirling with abandon across the orange shag rug

swan's market

they sell old dresses and raw red meat
blood and flesh and sweaty polyester
all
under the same roof what
more could you want?

*wounds heal
but scars are left behind*

i walk through the stalls
i try to re   member
wounds are just potential scars
they heal

*wounds heal
but scars are left behind*

the wound on my thigh
sizzles with hot pain

weeps milky tears
so much for browsing the stalls of swan's market
this meat needs to rest

i sit down and try to re   member

*wounds heal
scars are left behind*

re   member that chicks dig scars
as the infection burrows deeper in

tongue

i want a
poem to form
      under my
           tongue
                like a tiny brass key

so i can spit it out

water
    spilling
        down
           concrete
              steps

words inevitable as gravity

<untitled>

        embroidered on the body
        thorn in the heart
        ingrown
        scabbed over
        the kind of thing some people
        squeeze between two thumbs

day 48 covid pandemic

no one talks about
what a damned relief
an abortion can be

every woman i know
who knows what it's like
says the same thing

<untitled>

poets have bloodier teeth than you might expect

what it means to be a poet

it depends on who you ask

whether they've ever written one
                        or read one

or understand the itch to cobble words together &
                        wait

to see what happens on tongue and in ear
                        the page itself a kind of mind

when i encounter chaos on the blank page

leaning inward

        half of the ghost
        already given up i

                    consider
                        my
                    options

am bit

i am bit

ambition has long ivory teeth

curved like waning moons

dripping with slaver

better to mumble into your artisanal gin than to have ambition

better to walk 5 kilometers in shoes that leak in the sloppy rain

better to bite off your own fingers, one by one

ok, that last is a little extreme

(have you met me?)

i am bit

am bit

why poets are excluded from parties i

a young man   earnest, pink-cheeked
told me he
didn't have a shadow

i said nothing
afterall, what can be said to that?
i nodded
and smiled
and took
another sip
of my drink

he asked *how about you?*
being encouraging
in the way of pink-cheeked
young men with good manners

i thought and
thought

situation ratcheted to
maximum awkward

i settled on
i wear mine on the outside, like an unravelling
sweater

this did nothing to make things less awkward

why poets are excluded from parties ii

this is why people don't invite poets to parties
parched and pusillanimous
we partition people
into the profane and the puerile

i admit there can be other categories:
puppy-loving
pretendians
post-doctoral candidates
pedophiles
poodle enthusiasts
punk populists   and
prancing pricks   all come to mind

not sure if the pretty young man was profane or
puerile or merely

         a prancing prick

         but i know the flat lifeless eyes of a
         predator when i meet one

why aren't you famous she asked

do you mean actually famous or, like,
internet famous?

    is there a poetry famous?

only among other poets

    what about lit students

they read the canon of dead white men

    you got the colour right, at least

my eyebrows at maximum incredulity
        nevermind nevermind nevermind
        note: a polemic about casual racism
        from one whitewoman to another
        whitewoman
        has no business butting into this poem

                    no business whatsoever
                        another poem
                        for some other
                          time/space

but considering fame

 do not want:

        acclaim

        accolades
        applause
        celebration
        conspicuousity
        distinguishment
        eminence
        exaltation

not here for the:

        glory
        influence
        lionization (note: unless it is with
                            actual lions)
        might
        notoriety (note: actually, i do want
        that, sometimes, but only because i
        live a life of mind & spirit & desire to
        say "motherfucker" out loud in church,
        but nevermind nevermind nevermind)

that old intervention

that old intervention with the rising dead didn't work
    today
so they sit at my table with moon-pale mushrooms
growing from their faces along with their violence
their cowardice

meanwhile i'm chewing tinfoil
i don't even mind that much but i'm anxious not to
spit any sparks
that might start a fire i don't like to talk about it or
write about it

the incantations of language revivify those
miserable sons of bitches
better tinfoil on my tongue than the truth
i'm not ashamed
or afraid
just sad n' bored n' worried where the spark
might land after it flies from my mouth

sad
bc there is nothing in the past that can be changed

bored
bc trauma is the same old same old same
old common as dirt &
just as ancient

& worried because words
are powerful necromancy for restless memories i

need
a poem that can banish all the old husbands &
fathers back to hell where they belong

there is no need
to sit down and eat english muffins with them at
breakfast

just a game

implausible according to my arrogance
poet-mind is alive to it tho'

this is a game of the sims
created by game player we cannot know

it explains a lot
    casual cruelty
    actions determined through clickable menus
    presence of super-natural
    esoteric things[1]
    free will slider set
    to "moderate" not "high"

rosebud[2] motherlode[3]
never enough

kitchen needs renovation
rosebud motherlode

some more for a new dishwasher
ask for something else

have your sim take up sculpture[4]
rosebud motherlode

---

[1] If you have the correct expansion packs
[2] A Sims cheat code for free money
[3] Another Sims cheat code, for even more money
[4] An expensive hobby for a Sim

does knowing it's a game change anything? does our future-present digitization mean anything at all?

today

is cross-stitch an encryption key
and all the stitchers spies?

no matter

kneading bread same as breaking bones
will the hand that rocks
the cradle finally cradle the
rock?

is today the day?

unseen and

hidden things:

> who is unqualified
> > who is a soft touch
> > > who is blessed with voluptuous song
> > > > who is a gifted liar
> > > > > who pretends to like cold showers and
> > > > > > unbuttered Ryvita

who lives with a mourning that cannot be comforted

impermanence

woven into
the fabric of living
one moment
              the avocado is an uncleaved
baseball
the next
         a blackened paste

fluid

it's fluid they say i'm drowning in jelly i say i just
need somewhere
to stick my pole for
a little leverage it's fluid
they say you don't need a pole
says you i say i'm the one
who's drowning here i want just a sliver
of firm   dry   land.

enough for just one big toe i don't think it's too
much to ask and i can't be the only one who'd like
a small place to rest after   all things
mean things and while a thing can mean many
things there are   things it cannot and does
not mean there are limits
to the multiplicity of   meanings and though
they are tall broad and deep they are finite no one
              ever grew wings by wanting them bad
enough and a person with wings   can
be made to mean many (fluid and shifting) things
 but a person with wings is never a metaphor for a
plate of spaghetti and a nazi is always   a
fucking nazi so let's not get carried away with our
own cleverness in inventing   things surely
there is a bottom line or did i somehow miss it
when that
            bottom dropped out?

some might read this as a dog whistle for those
dull old binaries and
i suppose in the midst of all this jelly
that is something

                        you
                                can make this mean (if you
want, but why would you?)

                        my mind
keeps

                                        circling

                                        back

that big toe searching for a place to land.

where she's from

if she wears the dress i bought her outside
she's committing an offense against children

where she's from
when drag queens dress pretty and read to kids in
libraries they have to bring their own human
refrigerators with semi-automatic weapons

i wish i was kidding about that
it sounds like the kind of joke i'd tell
escalation into absurdity

but it's no joke:
- arizona
- arkansas
- missouri
- nebraska
- south carolina
- tenessee
- texas
- west virginia

i could go on

dead

i love her and i hold her
hand in public and forget
for a minute that
some people want her dead

50 truths i noticed after i turned 50

25. set out w/o a map
    just this compass
    rose on your palm

09. memory slips from one fiction
    to the next
    moments lost in story
    beginning middle end ::

37. some hurts don't stop

13. some women are powerful
    some women are dangerous
    some women collect things in miniature:
        ceramic ears of corn
        acorn hats for peanut-people
        bows stripped from bras
        plastic cats from bottles of cheap wine

some women are not where you expect them to be
never quite where you last left them

14. white ladies gals women womyn wimmin girls
    grrls macho chicks bar-room hot mamas
    nurses teachers healers hopers witches
    writers femmes butches bitches and all the
    white folks beyond the binary who may all the
    time or some of the time lean to the pink side
    of gender performativity:

let's knock it off

our genders don't xxx out our racism
4 the love of dog
        just admit it
                we are part of the
                    problem

15. I don't want to see pictures of your children

05. now a days
    to be heard
    you don't even
    need a body

18. i wonder for how
    much longer I will
    find fat stuffed olives
    or ripe strawberries
    out-of-season

24. desiccated strawberry hull sitting
    in my dirty sink
    flick it into the compost
    b/c my love's an apple core

39. he thinks I don't know
    he drinks my perfume
    when I'm gone

08. people shoplift a lot more than you'd think

02. on the finding of clitorises:
    front n' center is hard to find?

17. people lie to get sex
    they always have and they
    always will

21. closure is a well-intentioned fantasy

07. we shy away
    unblinkered horses
    eyes rolling white

11. we can't shop our way to the revolution

03. enough already with

                    indigo children
                    astrology
                    anti-vaxxing
                    sancti-mommying
                    purse dogs

14. god or no god
    the hole in my chest is real

    yearning
    velvet-furred cat arching
    just outofreach

    god or no god
    the mystery is real

20. the moment when
    worked through with paint
    the paper turns to cloth

        it doesn't last

10. without this hole in my chest
would i bother to
stretch toward
things out of reach

last red leaf
falling to loam

35. he sent himself to
lose himself in sacrifice to
himself,

it turns out,
as a way to save us from himself
in the first place
world without end

16. the poem begins

with any luck martians

won't tolerate a few rich white men
leaving earth
mars their freeze-dried fantasy
of self-salvation

the frogs aren't green any more
there are no oolichans in the river
loon calls sound unhinged and
cygnets die trembling deaths in lead-poisoned
ponds

many lives lived

white goose with arching neck &

discordant honk

peanut hidden in

unbreakable shell

sweet soft mama with milky

breasts & wet paintbrushes

otter, floating, holding a

warm smooth stone

day 49 covid pandemic

what can live in ice and fire?
murmurations
    sideways flying crow

dropped

you dropped to the pavement

                                       exhausted

not sure you could drink we offered

                                       sugar-water

gleaming green feathered throat

                                       swallowing

your curled tendril tongue found

                                       sweet & wet

flicker

intermittent taps
yellow beak on tin flashing
sun at apex

birbs are a lie

the internet says *birbs are a lie*
not yet not yet
but soon

there is a pretend conspiracy theory that birds
don't actually exist

birds, or *birbs* in internet-speak, are a false flag
perpetrated by them (whoever they are)
to fool us (whoever we are), all for some obscure
reason that furthers a dastardly plan

no

birbs are a lie is prophesy

in the 19th century, north american bird
populations were not measured by counting the
birdies but by
timing on your pocket watch how long the flock
blocked out the sky

carrier pigeons by the thousands

monumental murmuration
    of wings

carrier pigeons have gone the way of the dodo as has the dodo and the imperial woodpecker and many more besides

                                      bachman's warbler
                                                great auk[5]
                                    carolina parakeet[6]
                              ivory-billed woodpecker
                                          labrador duck
                                                  heath hen
                            dusky seaside sparrow[7]

---

[5] North American penguins
[6] North American parrots
[7] People built the Kennedy Space Center in the same area as this bird's only nesting ground, wiping them out.

neighbourhoods where i have lived
had crows and pigeons and wrens and starlings
and jays

how much longer
how many 45 °c (113 °f) days can they survive

hummingbirds–tiny warrior birds–are dying
from a region-wide bacterial infection
spread by the sugar-water we feed them

crows that live in the treetops near my place
hop across the dry grass
beaks open, panting

made and unmade over and over again, world without end
not that way now
                                        not
                                    anymore

i can see the end from where i stand like a
plume of wildfire smoke on the flame horizon
creeping nearer

forests catch on fire every
year for the past 17 years each
worse than the one before
every year *it's the worst year for wildfires in
recorded history* and we
speak of *wildfire season* like it's always been a
thing for any

youngsters in the back

it was not

also for the youngsters in the back
i know it sounds stupid and simplistic and paranoid

but

the world is run by narcissistic psychopaths
who will not learn　　　　　　　　　　and do
not care
because the anthropocene extinction
pardon me–the apocalypse–creates value

　　　　　　　　　　　　　　　　　　　for

shareholders

since every summer is now the hottest one on
record
that means
this summer is the coolest one you'll have for the
rest of your life

a few winters ago in
quebec there were towns colder
than any spot on mars

last week in spain the temp was
60° c (140° f)

old people and babies and unhoused people and every kind of

animal

dropping

dead

i get it no one

wants to be living
in interesting times

problem: we are tho'

so

i am made and unmade, world about to end

as we penguin-march into   i-know-not-what
taking
most other life with us

i think about the 5 other mass
extinction events & i
re   member about the anaerobic bacteria re
          starting things & i
think is it
            enough?

no

about the author

Chloe Cocking writes poetry, dark urban fantasy, fairy tales, and sternly-worded letters of complaint. She loves fancy shoes and all things caffeinated. She lives in Maple Ridge, B.C. with three humans, three cats, and one nervous rescue Yorkie. **world without end: poems** is her second book of poetry. Her other works, all on Filidh's imprint, include **Three's the Charm** (short stories, 2021), **Hector** (poetry, 2019), **Fables, Fictions, and Fantasies: A Compendium** (short stories, 2018), and **Blood Rain** (novel, fiction, 2017).

www.ingramcontent.com/pod-product-compliance
Lightning Source LLC
Chambersburg PA
CBHW071740040426
42446CB00012B/2409